To:

_____

From:

_____

Our mission is to publish and distribute inspirational products offering exceptional value and biblical encouragement to the masses.

NATURE'S PRAISE

Worship

Music and Inspiration to Celebrate the Outdoors

BARBOUR
PUBLISHING

All things bright and beautiful,

all creatures great and small,

all things wise and wonderful:

the Lord God made them all.

CECIL FRANCES ALEXANDER

Good heavens, of what uncostly
material is our earthly happiness
composed. . .if we only knew it.
What incomes have we not had
from a flower, and how unfailing
are the dividends of the seasons.

JAMES RUSSELL LOWELL

Some people, in order to discover God, read books. But there is a great book: the very appearance of created things. Look above you! Look below you! Read it.

St. Augustine

Nature is the art of God.

THOMAS BROWNE

Let the rivers clap

their hands,

let the mountains

sing together for joy.

PSALM 98:8 NIV

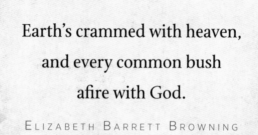

Earth's crammed with heaven,
and every common bush
afire with God.

ELIZABETH BARRETT BROWNING

Nature. . .unfolds her
treasures to [man's] search,
unseals his eye, illumes his
mind, and purifies his heart;
and influence breathes from
all the sights and sounds
of her existence.

ALFRED BILLINGS STREET

If people sat outside and looked

at the stars each night,

I'll bet they'd live

a lot differently.

BILL WATTERSON

*In the beginning
God created
the heavens and
the earth.*

GENESIS 1:1 NIV

Lie down and listen to

the crabgrass grow.

MARYA MANNES

To me a lush carpet of pine
needles or spongy grass
is more welcome than the most
luxurious Persian rug.

HELEN KELLER

The tulip and the butterfly

Appear in gayer coats than I:

Let me be dressed fine as I will,

Flies, worms, and flowers

exceed me still.

ISAAC WATTS

The best remedy for those who
are afraid, lonely, or unhappy is
to go outside, somewhere where
they can be quiet, alone with the
heavens, nature, and God.
Because only then does one feel
that all is as it should be.

ANNE FRANK

There is nothing in the world more peaceful than apple leaves with an early moon.

ALICE MEYNELL

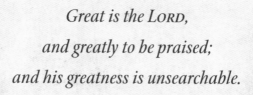

*Great is the L*ORD,

and greatly to be praised;

and his greatness is unsearchable.

PSALM 145:3 KJV

Art gallery? Who needs it?
Look up at the swirling
silver-lined clouds in the
magnificent blue sky or at the
silently blazing stars at midnight.
How could indoor art be any more
masterfully created than God's
museum of nature?

GREY LIVINGSTON

The trees are God's great
alphabet: with them He writes in
shining green across the world
His thoughts serene.

LENORA SPEYER

If the sight of the blue skies fills
you with joy, if a blade of grass
springing up in the fields has
power to move you, if the simple
things of nature have a message
that you understand, rejoice,
for your soul is alive.

ELEONORA DUSE

I praise You, O God,
for the marvelous works of Your hands.
For You alone are the Creator of
the heavens and earth.

LEE WARREN

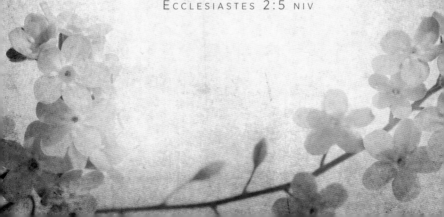

I made gardens and parks and planted

all kinds of fruit trees in them.

ECCLESIASTES 2:5 NIV

Lord, make us mindful of the
little things that grow and
blossom in these days to make
the world beautiful for us.

W. E. B. Du Bois

Climb a tree—
it gets you closer
to heaven.

UNKNOWN

I think that I shall never see

A poem as lovely as a tree.

A tree whose hungry mouth is prest

Against the earth's sweet flowing breast;

A tree that looks at God all day

And lifts her leafy arms to pray. . . .

JOYCE KILMER

Great things are done when men
and mountains meet.

WILLIAM BLAKE

For you make me glad by your deeds, Lord; I sing for joy at what your hands have done.

PSALM 92:4 NIV

All that I have seen teaches me to trust God for all I have not seen.

UNKNOWN

Earth laughs in flowers.

RALPH WALDO EMERSON

Nature is full of genius,
full of the divinity;
so that not a snowflake escapes
its fashioning hand.

HENRY DAVID THOREAU

I love to think of nature as an
unlimited broadcasting station,
through which God speaks to us
every hour, if we only tune in.

GEORGE WASHINGTON CARVER

When I look at your heavens,
the work of your fingers,
the moon and the stars,
which you have set in place,
what is man that you are mindful
of him, and the son of man
that you care for him?

Psalm 8:3–4 esv

Beauty puts a face on God.
When we gaze at nature,
at a loved one, at a work of art,
our soul immediately recognizes
and is drawn to the face of God.

MARGARET BROWNLEY

It is not so much for its

beauty that the forest makes

a claim upon men's hearts,

as for that subtle something,

that quality of air,

that emanation from old trees,

that so wonderfully changes and

renews a weary spirit.

ROBERT LOUIS STEVENSON

To find the universal
elements enough; to find the
air and the water exhilarating;
to be refreshed by a morning
walk or an evening saunter;
to be thrilled by the stars at night;
to be elated over a bird's nest or
wildflower in spring—
these are some of the rewards
of the simple life.

John Burroughs

Climb up on some hill
at sunrise. Everybody needs
perspective once in a while,
and you'll find it there.

ROBB SAGENDORPH

The path of the
righteous is like the
morning sun, shining
ever brighter till the
full light of day.

PROVERBS 4:18 NIV

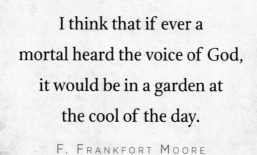

I think that if ever a
mortal heard the voice of God,
it would be in a garden at
the cool of the day.

F. FRANKFORT MOORE

You must not know too much,
or be too precise or scientific
about birds and trees
and flowers and watercraft;
a certain free margin,
and even vagueness. . .
helps your enjoyment
of these things.

WALT WHITMAN

God writes the Gospel not in the Bible alone, but on trees and flowers and clouds and stars.

MARTIN LUTHER

If you don't know what's meant
by God, watch a forsythia
branch or a lettuce leaf sprout.

MARTIN H. FISHER

Each little flower that opens,
each little bird that sings,
God made their glowing colors,
He made their tiny wings.

CECIL FRANCES ALEXANDER

But let all who take refuge in you be glad; let them ever sing for joy. Spread your protection over them, that those who love your name may rejoice in you.

PSALM 5:11 NIV

The human spirit needs places

where nature has not been

rearranged by the hand of man.

UNKNOWN

The sun is. . .warmth-giving

and happiness-giving. . . .

JESSI LANE ADAMS

The moon is like a
mystery novel, the sun like a
motivational self-help book,
and the stars a coffee-table
book of photography.
The sky is the whole library,
and God the librarian.

PEPPER GIARDINO

You will find something
more in woods than in books.
Trees and stones will teach you
that which you can never
learn from masters.

St. Bernard

I will send you rain in its season,
and the ground will yield its crops
and the trees their fruit.

LEVITICUS 26:4 NIV

There is
not a sprig of
grass that shoots
uninteresting
to me.

Thomas Jefferson

[Lord,] considering
Your concern for even the
sparrow brings joy to my soul
this day—knowing that You care
infinitely more for me.

LEE WARREN

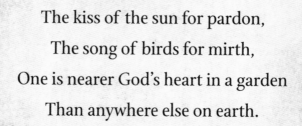

The kiss of the sun for pardon,

The song of birds for mirth,

One is nearer God's heart in a garden

Than anywhere else on earth.

D O R O T H Y   F R A N C E S   G U R N E Y

For in the true nature
of things, if we rightly consider,
every green tree is far more
glorious than if it were made
of gold or silver.

MARTIN LUTHER

By faith we understand that the universe was created by the word of God, so that what is seen was not made out of things that are visible.

Hebrews 11:3 esv

And this, our life. . .

finds tongues in trees,

books in the running brooks,

sermons in stones. . .

WILLIAM SHAKESPEARE

Forget not that the
earth delights to feel your
bare feet, and the winds long
to play with your hair.

KAHLIL GIBRAN

Whenever I see sunbeams
coming through the clouds,
it always looks to me like God
shining Himself down onto us.
The thing about sunbeams
is they're always there,
even though we can't see them.
Same with God.

ADELINE CULLEN RAY

[Heavenly Father,] help me to
never lose a sense of wonder over
the way You spoke the
world into existence.
Keep me in awe, Father,
as I consider how You've arranged
for the sun to rise each morning,
and for the ice to melt each spring,
and for the plants to
come back to life.

Lee Warren

Nature will bear the closest
inspection. She invites us to
lay our eye level with her
smallest leaf, and take an
insect view of its plain.

HENRY DAVID THOREAU

"I have set my rainbow in the clouds, and it will be the sign of the covenant between me and the earth."

GENESIS 9:13 NIV

If you've never been thrilled
to the very edges of your soul
by a flower in spring bloom,
maybe your soul has never
been in bloom.

AUDRA FOVEO

Let the earth bless the Lord;
yea, let it praise Him and magnify
Him for ever. O ye mountains
and hills, bless ye the Lord. . . .
O all ye green things upon the
earth, bless ye the Lord:
praise Him, and magnify Him for ever.

THE BOOK OF COMMON PRAYER

I remember a hundred lovely lakes,

and recall the fragrant breath of

pine and fir and cedar and poplar

trees. . . . Whenever the pressure of

our complex city life thins my blood

and benumbs my brain,

I seek relief in the trail;

and when I hear the coyote wailing

to the yellow dawn, my cares

fall from me—I am happy.

HAMLIN GARLAND

In wilderness I sense the

miracle of life. . . .

CHARLES A. LINDBERG

Sing for joy, you heavens,

*for the L*ORD *has done this;*

shout aloud, you earth beneath.

Burst into song, you mountains,

you forests and all your trees.

ISAIAH 44:23 NIV

Rather would I see daisies in
their thousands, ground ivy,
hawkweed, and even the. . .
plantain with tall stems,
and dandelions with splendid
flowers and fairy down,
than the too-well-tended lawn.

W. H. HUDSON

I thank You God for this
amazing day, for the leaping
greenly spirits of trees,
and for the blue dream of sky,
and for everything which is
natural, which is infinite,
which is yes.

E. E. CUMMINGS

Even if I knew that tomorrow
the world would go to pieces,
I would still plant my apple tree.

MARTIN LUTHER

I can enjoy society in a room; but out of doors, nature is company enough for me.

WILLIAM HAZLITT

To the Lord your God belong the heavens, even the highest heavens, the earth and everything in it.

Deuteronomy 10:14 niv

Beauty. . .
is the shadow of
God on the universe.

GABRIELA MISTRAL

How wonderful, O Lord,
are the works of Your hands. . . .
The beasts of the field,
the birds of the air bespeak Your
wondrous will. In Your goodness
You have made us able to hear
the music of the world,
a divine voice sings through
all creations.

TRADITIONAL HEBREW PRAYER

No site in the forest is
without significance,
not a glade, not a thicket that
does not provide analogies to the
labyrinth of human thoughts.
Who among those people with
a cultivated spirit,
or whose heart has been wounded,
can walk in a forest without the
forest speaking to him?

HONORÉ DE BALZAC

May flowers always line
your path and sunshine light your day.
May songbirds serenade you
every step along the way.
May a rainbow run beside you
in the sky that's always blue.
And may happiness fill your heart
each day your whole life through.

IRISH BLESSING

Let the trees of the forest

sing, let them sing

*for joy before the L*ORD*.*

1 CHRONICLES 16:33 NIV

Trees are happy for no reason;
they are not going to become
prime ministers or presidents,
and they are not going to
become rich, and they will never
have any bank balance.
Look at the flowers—for no reason.
It is simply unbelievable
how happy flowers are.

OSHO

We can learn a lot from trees:
they're always grounded but
never stop reaching heavenward.

EVERETT MAMOR

I am not bound for any public place, but for ground of my own where I have planted vines and orchard trees, and in the heat of the day climbed up into the healing shadow of the woods.

WENDELL BERRY

Once you have heard
the lark, known the swish of
feet through hilltop grass,
and smelt the earth made ready
for the seed, you are never again
going to be fully happy about
the cities and towns. . . .

GWYN THOMAS

I lift up my eyes to the hills.

From where does my help come?

My help comes from the Lord,

who made heaven and earth.

Psalm 121:1–2 esv

What is life?

It is the flash of a firefly in the night.

It is the breath of a buffalo in

the wintertime. It is the little

shadow which runs across

the grass and loses itself

in the sunset.

CROWFOOT

The cold wind in the winter,

the pleasant summer sun,

the ripe fruits in the garden:

God made them every one.

CECIL FRANCES ALEXANDER

The beauty of creation convinces me that the Creator not only loves me, but He wants me to have the very best.

UNKNOWN